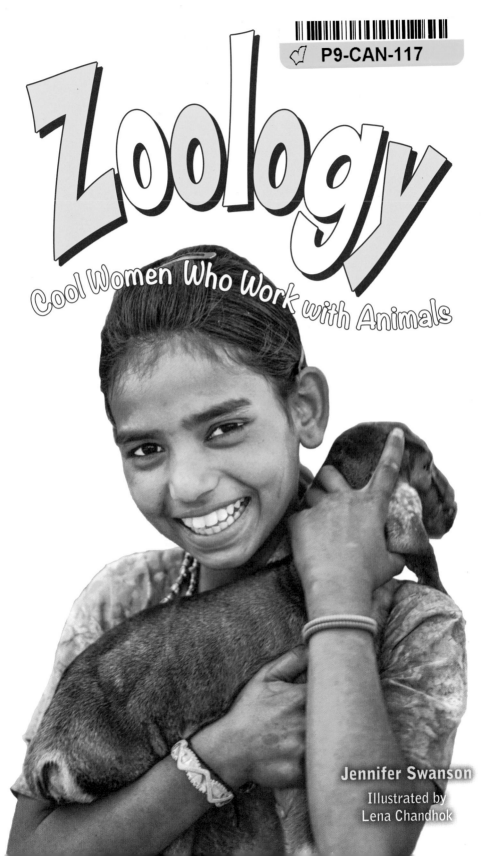

Zoology

Cool Women Who Work with Animals

Jennifer Swanson

Illustrated by
Lena Chandhok

Nomad Press
A division of Nomad Communications
10 9 8 7 6 5 4 3 2 1

This book was manufactured by CGB Printers,
North Mankato, Minnesota, United States
April 2017, Job #220015

ISBN Softcover: 978-1-61930-505-2
ISBN Hardcover: 978-1-61930-501-4

Educational Consultant, Marla Conn

Questions regarding the ordering of this book should be addressed to
Nomad Press
2456 Christian St.
White River Junction, VT 05001
www.nomadpress.net

Printed in the United States.

~ Other titles in the Girls in Science Series ~

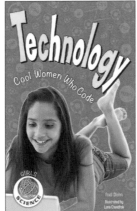

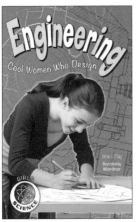

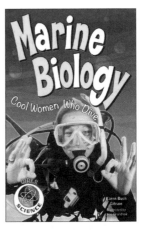

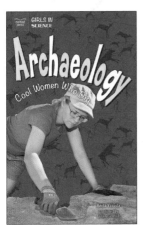

How to Use This Book

In this book you'll find a few different ways to explore the topic of women in zoology.

The essential questions in each Ask & Answer box encourage you to think further. You probably won't find the answers to these questions in the text, and sometimes there are no right or wrong answers! Instead, these questions are here to help you think more deeply about what you're reading and how the material connects to your own life.

There's a lot of new vocabulary in this book! Can you figure out a word's meaning from the paragraph? Look in the glossary in the back of the book to find the definitions of words you don't know.

Are you interested in what women have to say about zoology? You'll find quotes from women who are professionals in the zoology field. You can learn a lot by listening to people who have worked hard to succeed!

Primary sources come from people who were eyewitnesses to events. They might write about the event, take pictures, or record the event for radio or video. Why are primary sources important?

PS

Interested in primary sources? Look for this icon.

Use a QR code reader app on your tablet or other device to find online primary sources. You can find a list of URLs on the Resources page. If the QR code doesn't work, try searching the Internet with the Keyword Prompts to find other helpful sources.

CONTENTS

Let's Explore Zoology

Animals are everywhere. You can find them high in the sky, up in a tree, running through the forest, swimming deep in the ocean, and burrowed far under the dirt. They swim, crawl, fly, scoot, run, walk, and soar. Maybe you've tracked ants as they made a line across the sidewalk or followed the footprints of a rabbit or fox into the wilderness. Perhaps you've watched animals as they live and interact in a zoo.

Imagine being the one person who is responsible for raising a baby tiger. Sound interesting? Become a zoologist!

Zoology is the study of everything having to do with animals. Zoologists examine how and why animals look, act, and behave, in their environments and with other animals. There is much to learn about animals. Sometimes, learning about animals can teach us about ourselves—the human animal!

In *Zoology: Cool Women Who Work with Animals*, you will learn about three women who have made great strides in a field that has been around for hundreds of years. These women have faced many challenges and achieved success as zoologists through hard work and determination.

Studying zoology requires commitment, courage, and patience. Sometimes, it takes days just to capture a glimpse of a new animal in the wild or to see a flock of birds fly overhead. These women have all of these qualities and use them to improve their skills.

Stephanie Kim is a graduate student at the Queen's University Biological Station (QUBS), where she is finishing up her master's degree in zoology. She is collecting data on the interactions and natural history of song and swamp sparrows.

On her graduate field trips, she has experiences that she will never forget. These include seeing rattlesnakes and blue-footed boobies. She has held whiskered screech owls and eaten the freshest fruits from the trees on the way to the biology station.

Elise Newman currently works at the San Diego Zoo Safari Park as a zookeeper, primarily with tigers and lions. Before moving to San Diego, California, she was a zookeeper at the Binghamton Zoo at Ross Park in New York. She worked with a variety of animals, including tigers, red pandas, and river otters. Elise has also studied in Kenya and Tanzania, tracking elephants.

66 I was brought up to understand Darwin's theory of evolution. I spent hours and hours in the Natural History Museum in London looking at the descriptions of how different kinds of animals had evolved, looking at the sequence of fossil bones looking gradually more and more and more and more like the modern fossil. 99

—Jane Goodall,
primatologist, anthropologist,
expert on chimpanzees

Erin Seney has a PhD in wildlife and fisheries science. She currently works as an assistant research scientist with the University of Central Florida. Erin's research has involved tracking and observing marine turtles. She helped develop a safe and animal-friendly transmitter to attach to the turtles. Overall, she has done more than 14 years of sea turtle and ecological research in the field.

In this book, you'll read all about the challenges these zoologists have faced. You'll learn what types of animals they like to study and how they are constantly on the hunt for new information. Their stories might even inspire you to become a zoologist!

But first, let's take a look at how the field of zoology has developed throughout the years. After all, humans have been studying animals since we first appeared on the planet.

Ask & Answer

Why is zoology an important career for women and men? What would science be like if only one gender worked at it?

CHAPTER 1

Observing Animals

Zoology is a part of a science called biology. Biology simply means the study of living things. Biology can include plants, animals, and humans. Zoology is the study of the structure and make-up of animals—how they look, live, and interact with other species or groups. Zoologists also study how animals function in an environment. All kinds of animals are included in the field of zoology—snakes, whales, tigers, birds, elephants, and even cats and dogs.

A zoologist can study pretty much any type of animal they want. The science of zoology has been around for thousands of years. Humans have always wanted to learn more about animals.

Some zoologists study the entire organism. This means that they learn everything they can about a certain type of animal—how it sleeps, eats, and moves. They study its relationship with the world and other animals of its own species or different species.

Other zoologists study just a certain part of an organism. For example, a zoologist might be interested in how diseases develop and spread within a group of animals. Perhaps they want to know more about how the animal developed certain traits, such as eye color, hair color, and body size.

There are many names for zoologists. Some are called wildlife biologists and others are called cell biologists.

Ask & Answer

If you could pick any animal to study, what would it be? Would you want to study in a laboratory or go out into the field?

Some are named after the particular species they are studying. Entomologists study bugs. Herpetologists study snakes. Marine biologists study animals that live in the ocean.

Zoologists can also be classified by the type of work they do. A zoologist that works in an applied field is one who uses, or applies, a type of scientific knowledge to a specific problem.

An example of this is a zoologist who wants to learn more about how a population of bugs multiplies in the wild. They record the environmental factors, such as weather, temperature, how much food is available, and how predators affect the bugs.

Then, the zoologist takes that information and applies it to a different problem. Perhaps they need to know how to control the population of that bug. Too many bugs in one place could be bad for the trees or the crops that are being grown there.

A zoologist who works more in a pure field is one who is interested in increasing their knowledge about a certain animal. They study the animal completely to learn everything about it. These zoologists are not necessarily using the information for anything else, but simply want to observe and inform.

ZOOLOGY THROUGH THE AGES

The first zoologist to classify animals lived more than 2,000 years ago. Aristotle (384–322 BCE) is widely considered to be the "father of biology" and also zoology. While people studied animals before Aristotle, he was the first to separate them into groups.

One group was called "blooded" animals, which included four-footed animals, birds, and fish. The second group he called "non-blooded" animals and broke them down into mollusks, crabs, and insects. Aristotle recorded his results in nine different books.

These books were eventually published together and called *Historia Animalium, De Partibus Animalium and De Generatione Animalium*, better known as *The History of Animals*. Aristotle included every known animal at the time, including humans. He noted how and what they ate, their habitats, how they moved, and what they looked like.

While his observations were comprehensive—they filled nine books!—they were not always accurate. Still, Aristotle's book was used as the standard for zoologists going forward. It is considered to be the starting point for the field of zoology.

A few hundred years later, in 23 CE, Pliny the Elder worked as a soldier, lawyer, and writer. He wrote a series of books called *Historia Naturalis*, or *Natural History*.

This collection of 37 books included all of the observations he had made about the science of the world around him. Four of those books were on zoology.

Pliny included lots of random facts, most of which had gone previously unrecorded. His book was accepted and used as the standard for scientific thought for a thousand years. Although many of his theories were later proved to be wrong or incomplete, the books are still a great way to see how scientists thought in those days. They are also proof that a zoologist's best method of research is observing and recording what they see.

Pliny the Elder

Pliny the Elder's series of books is one of the largest to have survived from the time of the Roman Empire. He wrote it at night, after working during the day for Emperor Vespasian. He hadn't finished the series at the time of his death, but it was complete enough to be published and read by people interested in animal life. You can read the text here. How is the science used in the series different from the scientific method we use today?

Pliny the Elder *Natural History*

The biggest advance in zoology came in the 1700s, when physician and botanist Carl Linnaeus devised a system of classifying animals. This system is called taxonomy, or binomial nomenclature.

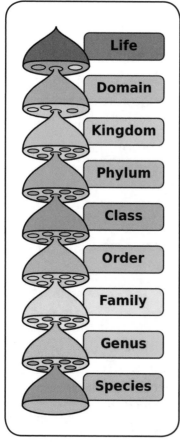

A diagram of the classification system of all living things

credit: Peter Halasz

Every living being is classified according to Linnaeus's chart. While that means that they all have many names, each animal is typically known by only two names—the genus and the species.

The genus is the general name of the animal family. The species is the specific name of the animal. For example, humans are known as *Homo sapiens*, where *Homo* is the genus name and *sapiens* is the species name. In Latin, *Homo sapiens* means "wise person."

If zoologists were talking about a bear, they would use the genus name *Ursus*. Each different bear would have a separate species name. A brown bear is called *Ursus arctos*. The American black bear is *Ursus americanus* and the polar bear is *Ursus maritimus*.

Linnaeus's system is so accurate that his names are still used by zoologists. He invented it just by observing and classifying, two tools all zoologists need!

EVOLUTION CHANGED EVERYTHING

In the 1800s, one of the most famous zoologists of all time, Charles Darwin, changed how all living things on Earth are viewed. A naturalist and geologist, he spent five years traveling around the world on the research ship HMS *Beagle*.

He studied plants, animals, and fossils from many different countries. Through his research and observations, he came up with a theory of how species had come to exist.

An illustration of the HMS *Beagle*
credit: R.T. Pritchett

The First Female Zoologist

Pythias of Assos is believed to have lived in the fourth century BCE and to have been the first female marine zoologist. She was the wife of Aristotle and helped him in his work creating an encyclopedia of animals. She is thought to have also collected many living animals herself.

Darwin believed that many species throughout the world were related. He noticed slight differences in animals due to their different environments. Still, they had many similarities. This caused him to conclude that animals evolve, or change over time.

Darwin assumed that the many different animals had come from the same ancestors. For example, today's Asian elephants might be descendants of the ancient woolly mammoths.

Darwin also believed that one species might be better equipped to survive than another. He called that theory "natural selection." He published his ideas in a book called *On the Origin of Species by Means of Natural Selection*.

The theory of evolution and ideas on natural selection changed zoology forever. It inspired and intrigued a great many zoologists. Darwin's book influenced them to ask questions and investigate to find answers. Those are great qualities that all zoologists need.

WOMEN IN ZOOLOGY

Women have made significant contributions to the study of zoology since ancient times. Not all of them have been recognized for their efforts.

In the last 100 years, that has changed dramatically. Today, more women than ever are becoming zoologists. They take rigorous classes at colleges and universities, go out into the field, and write scientific papers. Women speak at scientific conferences and forums and are held in great regard.

One woman, noted zoologist Dame Jane Goodall, was even knighted by the queen of England for her contributions to zoology.

As a child, Jane's father gave her a chimpanzee toy. It was so lifelike that some of her mother's friends were afraid it would scare Jane. Instead, this toy inspired her to follow her lifelong passion for animals.

Jane studied hard and, despite many obstacles, became a zoologist. She then set out on the greatest journey of her life. She went into the wilderness in Tanzania and lived with the chimpanzees.

> 66 As a small child in England, I had this dream of going to Africa. We didn't have any money and I was a girl, so everyone except my mother laughed at it. 99
>
> **—Jane Goodall**

Jane spent a long time getting the chimps to trust her. She used the tools of a zoologist—patience and observation. She visited the same group of chimpanzees every single day at the same time. She did this for an entire year. This got them used to her, so they began to allow her to come closer.

After she had been there for two years, Jane was able to approach the chimps and feed them bananas. Her waiting and patience had paid off! As Jane ate, slept, and lived with the chimpanzees, she learned much about them. She discovered that, like humans, they have different social groups. Chimps have their own communication system.

Most importantly, Jane witnessed the chimps make tools to help them gather food. This was a new discovery in zoology. Previously, zoologists believed that only humans make and use tools.

For the next 45 years, Jane devoted her life to learning about the chimpanzees and also to educating others about them. She became a champion of the environment and encouraged all nations, particularly in Africa, to take care of nature. She thought that they should limit the impact of tourism on the animals' habitats.

Jane has spoken out about the ethical treatment of animals and the intelligent use of research. She founded the Jane Goodall Institute and still works in support of animal conservation and social welfare projects.

As a result of all her efforts, Jane has received many awards and accolades. To think, all of this started with her love of a toy chimpanzee and her parents' encouragement to pursue her dreams.

Ask & Answer

What do you dream of doing? Does it include studying animals? How will you overcome any obstacles that come your way?

Dian Fossey
photo credit: The Dian Fossey Gorilla Fund International

Dian Fossey

Dian Fossey (1932–1985) grew up loving animals. At the age of six, she started horseback riding, which she would continue to do later in life. When she first went to college, Dian studied business. Her father encouraged her to do this, but she couldn't shake her love of animals. When she was older, Dian met Dr. Louis Leakey, the zoologist who had inspired Jane Goodall. He mentioned that working with the great apes was something that he wished to do. That was enough for Dian. She set out to do just that.

Jane Goodall has been followed by many other female zoologists. Dian Fossey is an American zoologist who spent 18 years studying gorillas. She lived among the gorillas in Rwanda, studying their patterns and behaviors.

Profiles of successful female zoologists are found in many newspapers, respected scientific journals, and books for all ages. Women run animal research facilities, zoos, and animal care centers and host television programs about animals.

Educational opportunities for women include working as university professors, in training programs, and in school, laboratory, and field positions.

Dian overcame many setbacks: lack of money for a trip to Africa, war in the country where she was studying, poachers who tried to capture or kill the gorillas. Yet, she never gave up. Eventually, Dian spent 20 years of her life living among the apes. She was truly dedicated to them and served as a role model to many female zoologists. Her life is chronicled in the movie, *Gorillas in the Mist*. "When you realize the value of all life, you dwell less on what is past and concentrate more on the preservation of the future."

According to a study conducted by Arizona State University in 2014, more than 60 percent of all biology majors in college are female. While not all of those women will become zoologists, those are encouraging numbers.

Every year, the number of women training to be zoologists increases, providing even more role models for young women who love science. They let us all know that girls, too, can pursue their dreams to study animals in the laboratory and in the field.

You don't need special training or even a zoo to witness zoology. Just go out into your own backyard. Grab a chair and get comfortable.

Take a look around. What do you see? Tiny ants marching across your patio. Small bees buzzing around your garden. A rabbit racing across the lawn to nibble grass.

Ask & Answer

Are you interested in studying animals? Does one species of animals capture your attention more than others? Do you want to know how an animal lives, acts, and behaves in nature?

Animals are all around you. Write down your observations and ideas in your journal. This is the first step to being a zoologist.

A ZOOLOGIST'S TOOLS

In ancient times, zoologists did not have many tools to study animals. Their main tool was observation. They would sit in place for long periods of time and watch how the animals behaved. They recorded their observations in a journal and used that information to write books and scientific papers.

Interestingly enough, that is what most modern zoologists do as well. The best way to learn about an animal is to watch how it interacts with its environments and with other species.

Today, however, technology can help zoologists collect information. Cameras and video recorders capture the animals in action. Scientists can track temperature, weather, and environmental conditions with satellites.

Zoologists have well-equipped labs to take samples, perform experiments, and keep animals close for observation. Computers are used to collect and analyze data, create charts, identify patterns, and make predictions.

Young Zoologist

Anyone can be a zoologist. At the age of seven, Enzo Monfre knew that he loved animals. He wanted to share his passion for animals with others. He wanted to have his own zoology show. But how? His parents supported Enzo's dream and helped him figure it out.

Enzo started filming short videos of animals in their natural habitats. He uploaded his videos to YouTube and narrated them himself. It worked! Many people viewed Enzo's videos. Now, three years later, Enzo has gained some support. He has been on national television and radio programs. He has worked with the U.S. Fish and Wildlife Service and even done programs with the National Aeronautics and Space Administration (NASA). He established a company called Enzoology that brings fun zoology education to kids all around the world. You can check out his work at this website.

Enzoology 🔍

Some zoologists even use remotely operated vehicles deep under the sea to capture information about new species. The technology that today's zoologists have to help them is way beyond just a pencil and a notebook.

ZOOLOGY CAREERS

Zoologists study many different kinds of animals. As a zoologist, you might go on an expedition to Africa to study how elephants problem-solve or you might track bird migrations. You could take care of tigers at a zoo. You might even study how climate change can affect underwater creatures.

Zoologists work in zoos, research stations, universities, and laboratories. They go out into the wild to study animals in their own habitats, the place in nature where they live.

Sometimes, that means a zoologist will work on a ship or dive deep under the water to explore unique sea creatures. Perhaps they are camping in the forest to watch bears or coyotes.

Zoologists might even trek up mountains to see animals in their high-altitude homes. Any of these careers and many, many more are options that you could choose. So where do you start?

To become a zoologist, you need to study all different kinds of science. In high school, you can take biology, chemistry, ecology, and even physics courses. Writing and speech classes are important, too. As a zoologist, you need to have good communication skills because you will be writing scientific papers and presenting them to others. Zoologists also need to take math and statistics classes in order to do complex data analysis.

In college, you can take zoology, wildlife biology, and ecology. You may even be able to pick a class that focuses on a certain species, or group, of animals. If you like birds, you could take ornithology. If you like snakes, you might take herpetology. More math and writing classes will help you compute and create excellent presentations of all the data you will collect.

Get Involved

You can start pursuing your interest in zoology right now. Volunteer at the local zoo. Or just go there to observe the animals. Take a notebook and write down everything you see: how they eat and how they interact with others of their species or other animals. Organize your data. You might be surprised at what you learn!

You can gain experience by volunteering at your local zoo. Or you can help out at a veterinarian's office. Just living and working outdoors gives you valuable experience. You can begin your zoologist career at home by raising your own pets and observing their behaviors.

Use your critical thinking skills to figure out the habits of your pets and make notes of any changes you see. Observing, waiting, and learning—these are all great qualities that a zoologist must have.

Within the last 50 years, technology has enabled many more people to be introduced to zoology. Famous zoologists, such as the late Steve Irwin, better known as the "Crocodile Hunter," and Chris and Martin Kratt, also known as the "Wild Kratt Brothers," have brought zoology into our homes. Their television programs have captured animals in their own habitats, living, eating, and interacting with humans.

Let's meet three amazing women who are pursuing their own careers in zoology—Stephanie Kim, Elise Newman, and Erin Seney.

CHAPTER 2
Stephanie Kim

Stephanie Kim has lots of questions about the world. From the time she was young, she wanted to learn more about animals and nature. As a graduate student at Queen's University in Kingston, Ontario, Canada, she is pursuing her dream of a life spent in the field of zoology. Her passion is to discover everything she can about animals and nature and then to share her knowledge with others through teaching.

Stephanie Kim was born near Toronto, Ontario, in the Canadian province north of the Great Lakes. Toronto is on the shore of Lake Ontario and has more than 1,500 parks and a large number of rivers and ponds. Her parents encouraged Stephanie and her sisters to spend a lot of time outside.

Their house backed up to one of those parks, and Stephanie was always playing there with her sisters. They would run along the small brook and across the big fields, searching for wildlife. If she was lucky, she'd see a red fox, a white-tailed deer, or even a beaver.

WONDERING ABOUT THE WORLD

Like any budding scientist, Stephanie discovered that asking questions is one of the best ways to learn things. Her first real memory of her interest in animals happened at a young age.

When she was in first grade, her class went on a field trip to a nature center. The class was given some clear glass jars to use to collect water samples from the lake. They weren't looking for anything in particular— the idea was just to introduce science to the young first-graders.

At first, Stephanie wasn't very impressed. She remembers lying on the dock that stretched out into the lake, leaning over the edge, taking big scoops of water. It was hard to see through the murky water. Bits of plants, a few bugs, and maybe some leaves were all she could find. Not that exciting!

But then she caught something in her jar. A tadpole! A tiny little animal with a big head and a long tail. It swam around and around in the murky water, its gills moving in and out very quickly.

Stephanie was fascinated by the small animal that would one day become a frog. She was excited, and her mind was immediately filled with questions: What kind of frog will this end up being? How long will it be a tadpole? What does a tadpole eat?

All of these questions and more came pouring out of her. Stephanie had to know all she could about the creature that was swimming around in her mason jar.

Stephanie took her jar over to her teacher and began asking all of her questions. Even many years later, Stephanie remembers this day as the time she got her first taste, and love, of nature and science. And she has never forgotten how amazed she was that her teacher knew the answers to so many of her questions!

Ask & Answer

What activities do you love to do now? Do you ever think that they might lead you to a certain career?

> 66 It is a gift when someone can challenge you can open your mind to new ideas. 99

—Terri Irwin,
naturalist

Stephanie's mind buzzed with questions about the world around her. She was especially curious about the animals she saw in the park behind her house and in the streams and ponds.

Encouraged by her parents to continue loving animals and the outdoors, Stephanie's favorite days were when she went fishing with her father. They would go on special father-daughter trips to their secret spot and spend hours trying to catch fish. They used crayfish as bait. Some days, they didn't catch much. But even then, Stephanie would sit back and imagine all the different types of fish they might have caught—carp, trout, bass, or salmon.

She wondered if they'd catch more fish if they used different bait. Perhaps different times of the year would bring one type of fish more than another to her pole. She wondered many things about the fish in that pond.

These days helped shape her love of nature and animals. They also helped bring her closer to her family.

PASSION TO LEARN

Despite her love of animals, Stephanie always thought she would grow up to be a doctor. Her family was very science-oriented, but most of them were interested in human biology and medicine—how people worked, not animals. All through grade school and the first two years of high school, Stephanie believed that pursuing a career in medicine was what she was going to do.

That all changed when she stepped into her 11th-grade science class. Her high school science teacher made science fun! Stephanie loved hearing about the fieldwork he did on the island of Kauai during graduate school.

One of the Hawaiian Islands, Kauai is known as the Garden Isle because it is covered with rainforests and flowers. Stephanie's teacher made his experiences come alive for the students by describing beautiful images of waterfalls, tropical forests, and all of the different types of animals he saw.

Ask & Answer

Are you willing to change your mind to follow your own path? Even if it takes you in a different direction from your original one?

The Hawaiian island of Kauai

Not completely understanding why, Stephanie desperately wanted to go to Kauai to discover its unique environment. What Stephanie felt and responded to was her teacher's passion for learning.

Stephanie had that feeling, too, deep inside. It would come out again and again throughout her career as she learned new and interesting things. Stephanie's need to ask questions and have them answered was leading her toward her future.

66 Science makes people reach selflessly for truth and objectivity; it teaches people to accept reality, with wonder and admiration, not to mention the deep awe and joy that the natural order of things brings to the true scientist. 99

—Lise Meitner,
physicist

CHOOSING HER PATH

Stephanie didn't fully commit herself to pursuing a career in zoology until she entered college. She began her freshman year at Queen's University as a biology major. Biology is the study of life and living organisms. It is quite a broad topic and can cover everything from plants to animals to humans.

Stephanie was not very happy with the basic biology classes required for her first two years at school. She longed to learn more.

Donna Ball

It's never too late to follow your love of science, even if you've already started doing something else. Ask Donna Ball. She knows. As a teenager, Donna wanted to go to college to study science, but her father told her that college was a waste of time. He said that, instead, she should get married and raise a family. Donna did that, but her dream of getting a college degree never left her. When she was in her early 40s, Donna went to speak with a college counselor about starting her degree. He encouraged her to become a secretary, an easy job for a 40-year-old. Since she had been out of school for 20 years, she did not have the confidence to challenge him. At least, not at first. Donna took a required introductory math class. And she loved it!

She had many questions that were not being answered. She kept going, though, hoping to find the passion she'd had for science in high school.

At the beginning of her third year in college, Stephanie was finally able to find courses that really interested her. She took her first class on animal behavior and she loved it! She spent the entire semester, half of the school year, learning how scientists study animals in the field. Her passion from her days spent running through the park, playing at the pond, and fishing with her father was rekindled.

That fueled Donna's determination. This was her time to follow her dream! She switched her major to environmental science. She completed her four years in college to get a bachelor's degree and then went on to get a master's degree. Donna is now working at Save the Bay, an organization that helps to save and restore the tidal marsh of San Francisco Bay in California. As she says, "You must never give up on challenging yourself and being open to pursuing new dreams or changing directions."

Stephanie remembered her high school teacher's excitement for his study in Kauai. Her interest in zoology began to grow.

In her senior year in college, she finally took a class that changed everything for her. It was taught by an instructor whose thirst for knowledge was as great as Stephanie's. His enthusiasm for the science of biodiversity was contagious! Stephanie felt herself being drawn in.

Suddenly, all of Stephanie's questions were starting to find answers, or at the very least, connections. The biodiversity classes that discussed broad, global patterns of animals on the planet also helped to explain how they were all interconnected to the earth. It was a topic that she had never even known existed and one that she found endlessly fascinating.

To have an instructor with such an eagerness to pass on his knowledge was inspiring to Stephanie. She took in every word with great interest. As she says, "It was in these classes that I was introduced to really tough questions that have been asked for centuries, that scientists are still trying to answer!"

Biodiversity

Biodiversity is the entire web of animals, plants, and other organisms found on Earth. All of these things are interconnected by where and how they live, work, and exist. Think of it like a giant puzzle, where every piece has its place, but it must fit into the correct position to match on all sides.

Biodiversity can be studied on a global level or within a particular environment or ecosystem. For example, scientists who study biodiversity might look at how one fish fits in with all of the inhabitants of a pond, a lake, the ocean, or the world. It all depends on the perspective of the person who is performing the study. Here is a great video to describe biodiversity. Why is biodiversity so important?

Conservationbytes biodiversity 🔍

Stephanie had found her true calling. It may have taken her a long time—all the way until her fourth year in college—but she now knew what she wanted to be. Stephanie wanted to become a zoologist.

JUMPING INTO ZOOLOGY AND EDUCATION

Once Stephanie realized that zoology was what she really loved, she chose college courses that inspired and interested her. One of those was a class on conservation biology. Conservation biology is the study of all of the different ecosystems of the earth and how we as humans can work to protect animals and their habitats from being destroyed. It encourages people to consider Earth as a system that is all interconnected.

One species, or group, is connected to another when they share the same living space or habitat. Think of a giant web where all of the plants and animals in the world are connected.

Stephanie was drawn to the idea that the care and keeping of the forests, oceans, and land is the responsibility of every person on the planet. She was excited to work on her senior project about creating awareness of local conservation issues. Stephanie's group focused on how invasive species are harmful to the ecosystem.

What Is an Invasive Species?

An invasive species in an area is any living organism that was not originally born or planted in that area. Invasive species can take over an ecosystem and push other natural animals or plants out. For example, in the Everglades National Park in Florida, Burmese pythons, one of the largest snake species in the world, are now growing and living there. That is strange, since the pythons originally came from a small region in southeast Asia. How did the snakes get there? Apparently, they were once owned as pets by people who lived in Florida. When the snakes got too large, some people released them into the Everglades.

The snakes found the climate to their liking, so they have lived and thrived there ever since. The problem with having these snakes in the Everglades is that they eat many different birds and small animals there. The bigger pythons have even been known to eat alligators! This disrupts the ecosystem because there aren't any predators that will eat the pythons. So the pythons just keep eating and growing. Some of them have grown up to 20 feet long. The only way to get rid of them is to have zoologists remove them and place them in zoos.

Stephanie's research group dealt with the invasive species in the area where she lived in Canada. Since her goal was to increase awareness, she helped to create a game that they could use to inform students about the problem.

Stephanie and her group traveled to a local elementary school and spent the afternoon talking to the students and playing the game. For Stephanie, it was an amazing experience! She was finally able to tie together her love of science and her love of education. Taking what she had learned about invasive species, she was able to get kids involved in doing something about it. It was her turn to be the teacher that inspired the students.

Stephanie knew that zoology was where she wanted to be, so she decided to continue her studies. She enrolled in a graduate program to get her master's degree.

Ask & Answer

Is there a topic that you are passionate about? What can you do to tell people about it? How can you get others involved in helping?

Stephanie doing field research

INTO THE FIELD

Many zoologists will spend some amount of time outdoors, or "in the field," as it is called. When they are in the field, they are doing field research. This means they are collecting information about their subjects outside of a laboratory or classroom.

Why do zoologists do fieldwork? Because that is where the animals are! Zoologists need to see the animals in their own habitats, or environments, where they live, eat, and breed. They need to see the types of weather the animals endure, where and how they hunt for food, and the predators that might threaten them. For many zoologists, this is the best part of their job.

Stephanie felt that way when she conducted her first field research study. As a graduate student at Queen's University Biological Station (QUBS) in Ontario, Stephanie was a research assistant along with three other students in the field research crew.

Her job was to collect data on song and swamp sparrows. These are tiny birds that are found in or near wetlands, which are areas of land that are soaked with water. This might be a marsh, or edges of a pond or lake, or even open spaces with small shrubs or trees.

Stephanie and her fellow research assistants were tasked with capturing the sparrows and putting bands on their legs. The bands are a way of identifying the birds. To do this, they had to be very quiet and observe the birds from afar. They needed to see the territory in which the birds lived.

Then, when the birds were not around, the students set up mist nets near the shrubs. Mist nets are big pieces of mesh netting, something like a net used for tennis or volleyball. Mist nets are soft and have tiny holes. When the birds fly into the netting, they bounce off and become tangled in the mesh pocket below. The researcher then gently removes the birds, weighs them, and places the bands on their legs. Then, each bird is released back to the air.

The ornithologists, scientists who study birds, were trying to learn all they could about how the sparrows behave in the wild. Once the birds were banded, the researchers tried to find the cleverly hidden sparrows' nests.

A female golden-crowned kinglet in a mist net, before a band is placed on its leg and the bird is released.

Then came the most important part of field work—the waiting and the observing. Stephanie and her crew sat for hours watching the sparrows fly into and out of their nests. They wrote down everything they saw in their field notebooks.

Stephanie was thrilled to watch as the adult birds took care of the eggs. Then, the baby birds hatched. She wrote in her notebook, "They look like angry old men before they start developing feathers and start to look like birds!" The researchers watched the babies get bigger, their tiny beaks raised to the sky as the mother birds fed them.

Stephanie's crew stayed with the birds for the entire season, tracking and watching them. Learning so much about one particular species was the highlight of Stephanie's career. She says it was one of the most fun summers she has ever had!

FORGING AHEAD

Full of enthusiasm, Stephanie started her own research project to complete her master's program. To come up with a project for your master's degree, you need to have a really great question. Not a problem for Stephanie. She is always full of questions.

Since she had really enjoyed her field research study on the sparrows, Stephanie decided birds were pretty cool.

She wanted to learn more about them, especially their beaks. So, her research project was to figure out things that might affect the size of a bird's beak.

She describes it here:

> Imagine you and a friend are the exact same height. You go into a room and there's one piece of candy on a table and one piece of candy on a high shelf. If you're both the same height, you might fight over the candy you can both reach, but if one person is much taller, they can reach the candy on the high shelf and the other person can eat the candy from the table. Sometimes, animals do something very similar—they will evolve differences between each other so they don't have to fight over the same resources.

66 I was trying to figure out if birds from all over the world evolve differences in their bills (or beaks) so that they don't have to fight for things when they live with other birds. 99

Museums

If you can't get out into the field, the next best place to visit is a museum.

Museums are incredible sources of information! They have cool exhibits, including displays of animals, ecosystems, and plants. They are also filled with history on many different topics. Many museums have summer programs where you can do hands-on activities. Maybe you can even spend the night! Museums are amazing places filled with people who love science and history and who are all specialists in their fields. Here are a few museums to check out.

- Exploratorium in San Francisco, California
- Boston Children's Museum in Boston, Massachusetts
- Morrison Planetarium at the California Academy of Sciences in San Francisco
- National Museum of Mathematics in New York, New York
- The Leonardo in Salt Lake City, Utah
- Discovery Place Science in Charlotte, North Carolina

To find the answer to her question, Stephanie traveled to museums across the United States and Canada. She took pictures of the birds in the museums, and even got some scanned photos of them from other scientists. She began to compare the birds, taking notes along the way.

When she came up with her conclusions, she wrote them down in a very long paper called a thesis. At the time this book was written, Stephanie was still writing. When she is done, she will present it to her professors. It can take a long time to write a master's thesis. In the end, Stephanie will receive her master's degree.

LOOKING TO THE FUTURE

What's up next for Stephanie? She is not quite sure. She knows that she wants to continue her career as a zoologist. Will she go back into the field as a researcher? Go on to get her doctorate, or PhD, in zoology? Or perhaps become a teacher? She doesn't know yet, but teaching will most likely be in her future.

When Stephanie is teaching, she really loves sharing her knowledge with others. She remembers what it was like to be young and full of questions. She remembers the burning desire to have her questions answered, and to look to a teacher for the response.

Cool Careers: **Wildlife Rehabilitator**

Have you ever seen an injured animal and wondered how to help? Call a wildlife rehabilitator. They are specially trained zoologists who care for sick, injured, or even orphaned animals. The animal is carefully captured by the zoologist and transported to their laboratory or facility. There, the animal is treated for its injuries, fed, and taken care of until it can be released back into its natural habitat.

Stephanie might decide that she is just the teacher to answer all those questions and to encourage further learning. She would be thrilled to inspire more young people to become scientists, just as her family and her teachers inspired her.

66 We need visible female role models, willing to engage, share their experiences, . . . to ensure women's representation in science improves, and goes from strength to strength. Everyone knows the world needs science. Many acknowledge that science needs women. Let's make it possible for science to get the women it needs. 99

—Dr. Nathalie Pettorelli and Dr. Seirian Sumner,
research fellows at the Institute of Zoology

CHAPTER 3

Elise Newman

Do you love being outdoors? Do you have a passion for animals? Perhaps you want to learn more about how humans fit in the world among all of the plants and animals. Maybe you're like Elise Newman. She is a zookeeper who takes care of captive animals to ensure the survival of their species. She is also passionate about teaching people about conservation and protecting the natural resources of our planet.

47

Elise Newman has loved animals her whole life. She was that kid who always wanted more pets.

Her father was the same way when he was young. He was always bringing home frogs, spiders, and any other living thing he could stuff into his pockets. The more pets, the better. Like father like daughter!

At an early age, Elise convinced her parents that she was able to take care of many different kinds of pets. She had a dog, a fish, a bird, and even a turtle. Her parents were very supportive. They encouraged Elise in her love of animals and said yes to most of the animals she wanted. That is, until she decided that she wanted a hamster.

Her mother, Patricia, was not too keen on hamsters. They were smelly and reminded her of large rodents. But still, Elise's mom didn't want to discourage her daughter's love of animals, so she came up with a plan.

She told Elise that hamsters require special care that takes a lot of time and effort. Elise would need to learn about their care and be able to explain how she would take care of the hamster before she could get one. Elise's mom thought that maybe the idea of extra work would change Elise's mind about getting a hamster.

It didn't. In fact, the challenge made Elise more determined than ever. She went to the library and checked out every book she could find on hamsters.

She learned that hamsters need big cages filled with soft bedding materials, which are made from natural plant fibers. Hamsters should be handled gently, because if they are startled, they will bite. Hamsters are nocturnal, meaning that they are awake at night.

Elise gobbled up all of these facts. She loved learning all about hamsters. In her eagerness to share her newfound knowledge, she spouted facts about hamsters whenever and wherever she could. She realized that she wanted to grow up to be someone who taught people about animals.

And, yes, she did get her hamster.

Elise's love of animals was not confined to just household pets. She grew up in a suburb in California, but her parents drove her to a ranch twice a week so she could ride horses. In elementary school, she was a member of 4-H, a global organization that encourages kids to learn about animals by raising them and showing them in competitions.

Elise spent a lot of time working with her horse. She trained the horse to do different tricks, but it wasn't just about teaching him tricks. Elise brushed the horse, cleaned out his stall, and gave him food and water. Elise was happiest when she was taking care of animals, and she loved every second of it. But she wanted to learn more.

In fifth grade, Elise had an amazing science teacher— Mr. Harrington. She describes Mr. Harrington as being "outdoors-y," meaning that he loved to take his students outside. Some days he would even teach class outdoors.

> 66 I don't work at something because I think it's important. I work at things that, to me, are interesting. 99
>
> **—Eugenie Clark,**
> zoologist, nicknamed "The Shark Lady"

Mr. Harrington took his students on many field trips. Once, they went to Yosemite National Park for an overnight camping trip. They also went to many local nature centers and parks. He encouraged students to notice the rock formations, streams, plant life, and, of course, the animals they encountered on their hikes.

When they got back to class, the students wrote reports and gave presentations on what they'd seen. Mr. Harrington talked about the importance of conservation and keeping parks clean and safe for animals. Part of his message was that watersheds, or areas where water runs off the mountains onto the land, are valuable places where ecosystems thrive.

He instilled in Elise and his other students an eagerness to explore and learn more about the nature and animals in their own communities. And, of course, Elise's father, who loved all these things, too, was a parent volunteer for every one of Mr. Harrington's field trips.

Ask & Answer

Do you have a teacher or parent who supports what you are interested in? Do they inspire you to want to pursue your dreams? How does that make you feel?

A CHANGE OF DIRECTION

Elise knew she loved the outdoors and animals, but she had many questions. She started going to the veterinarian's office with her parents when it was time to take their dogs for their shots.

She talked to the veterinarian and asked many questions. The whole time, she was storing away the answers in her head. Elise thought that maybe one day she'd like to be a veterinarian and take care of animals.

A few years later, before college, she got the chance to try that out. Elise started volunteering at her local vet's office. As an assistant technician, she was in charge of helping calm the animals during their shots and when they had X-rays. She assisted the vets with surgeries.

Elise liked her job, but she also saw a lot of sick animals. She had never really thought about that. Most of the animals that Elise had dealt with until then were healthy and happy.

Ask & Answer

Have you ever had a job that you didn't like? Did you learn anything from it?

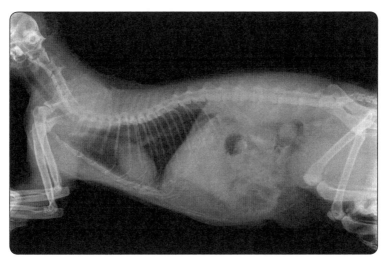

What animal do you think is being X-rayed?

Hint: meow!

She had always thought that since she loved working with animals, she would become a veterinarian. Seeing so many sick animals made Elise reconsider that path.

For Elise, working as a veterinary assistant was an eye-opener. She learned what she did not want to do with animals. She preferred to work with healthy animals, not ones that had just had surgery. She wanted the animals to be happy to see her, not scared that they had to visit the vet.

Sometimes, learning what you don't want to do is the first step to discovering what kind of career you do want to pursue.

What Do Animals Think About Vets?

Most animals know when they are going to the veterinarian's office. Vets aren't sure how animals know—it might be the smell, sounds, or location. Animals know they will be handled, weighed, and maybe even given shots. Vets do know that most animals don't like going there. The animals at the zoo even know when a veterinarian comes to visit them in their enclosure. It is not certain if it is because they smell differently or if it's because the vets don't interact with the animals on a daily basis.

Regardless, some of the animals react with fear when they see the vets. They hide in their cages or refuse to go into the examination rooms. They have even been known to throw their feces at a vet. Not a fun thing! It's hard to convince an animal that you are just there to help them. They can't understand what you are saying. What are some ways you can show animals that you only want to help them?

NOW WHAT?

While Elise was working at the veterinarian's office, she applied to pre-veterinary programs at colleges so she could study to become a vet. But after her hands-on experiences, she felt that was no longer what she wanted to do.

She still loved animals and had a strong passion to work with them in some way. What was the next step? Elise decided to try volunteering at the Sacramento Zoo in Sacramento, California. It made sense. Where would you go to see a bunch of different animals? Why, the zoo, of course!

It was the best decision she ever made. Elise loved working at the zoo. It was difficult work! Elise's job was to do all of the hands-off jobs for the zookeepers so that they could have more time with the animals. That meant a lot of cleaning.

First, Elise cleaned the empty enclosures by scooping all of the dirty, heavy hay into a wheelbarrow and disposing of it. The hay didn't smell too great since it usually contained animal feces. Not a fun job, but someone had to do it!

Then, she had to spread new hay on the floors of the enclosures. Elise was responsible for cleaning all of the glass in the reptile house. After all, the grubby handprints and nose prints prevented people from seeing the animals.

Elise spent many hours in the hot, California sun lugging hay, scooping poop, and wiping down glass. And she couldn't have been happier.

At the zoo, she asked lots of questions. She asked if she could follow the zookeepers around. She asked them about their training and about how they learned to take care of the animals.

Elise with a red panda at the Binghamton Zoo

> 66 The more clearly we can focus our attention on the wonders and realities of the universe about us, the less taste we shall have for destruction. 99

—Rachel Carson,
zoologist

Her persistence paid off when she was able to meet a few of the animals. But her favorite part was just sitting and watching them—the tigers, lions, elephants, and giraffes. Even the birds and the monkeys. She loved them all. By sitting and watching, Elise learned their behaviors, how they acted and interacted with each other and humans.

The time spent at the Sacramento Zoo was priceless. Elise now knew what she wanted to do with her life— become a zoologist!

BECOMING AWARE OF HOW YOU FIT INTO THE WORLD

Once Elise knew that she wanted to work with animals in the wild or in a zoo, she decided to take a class with Dr. Sara Pritchard on the ethics of biology. This class was about the role humans have in the environment of the world.

Dr. Sara Pritchard discussed how using fossil fuels, such as gasoline, natural gas, and coal, can cause the climate of the earth to change. She introduced her students to the idea of conservation, how humans need be aware of how they change the environment. For example, humans can protect the land and animals from the damaging effects of construction. Elise was fascinated by this topic.

Every zoologist you will meet in this book, as well as many others, are passionate about both animals and the environments the animals live in. Conservation is always a part of the discussion.

Habitats are constantly in danger from human intervention, weather, and climate change. Humans cut down trees to build houses, which cause the animals that live there to have to relocate. Wind, heavy rains, and temperature changes can affect ecosystems by eroding soil or damaging plants and trees. This affects all of the organisms that live there.

The Grand Canyon, a result of erosion

Five Organizations Involved in Conservation

1. Be Out There: Organized by the National Wildlife Foundation, this program encourages kids to get outside and experience nature. nwf.org/What-We-Do/Kids-and-Nature.aspx

2. Let's G.O.! (Get Outside): A program organized by the Children and Nature Network that combines play, service, and celebration to get kids actively involved in natural restoration projects. childrenandnature.org/initiatives/letsgo

3. REI Family Adventures: A program that promotes outdoor family events by providing organized hiking and biking activities as well as a variety of outdoor school courses. rei.com/adventures/familylanding.html

4. Sierra Club Outdoors: The Sierra Club organizes hiking, skiing, paddling, bird-watching, and conservation-oriented activities. content.sierraclub.org/outings/sierra-club-outdoors

5. Ocean Guardian Classrooms: Get your school involved in this program organized by the National Oceanic and Atmospheric Administration. sanctuaries.noaa.gov/education/og_classroom/welcome.html

Being aware of what humans are doing and taking into account the affect they have on the environment is important. It is possible for people to work to ensure that animals and humans coexist peacefully and happily.

Elise was so interested in this topic that she changed her major to environmental conservation and wildlife management. With that choice she got one step closer to her dream job!

IN THE FIELD

Like most budding zoologists, Elise found an opportunity to participate in field research. She was eager to get back outside to do what she loved—study animals.

Her first field research assignment was banding birds near Appledore Island in the state of Maine. It was a college field course, which means that, as a college student, she was not being paid to help the lead researchers.

Elise gained valuable insight into how research in the field is conducted. She also learned a great deal about all the different types of songbirds she helped to band.

Another part of her job was to count the seagulls that she saw. She and her fellow students were responsible for finding the seagull nests and, without disturbing them, counting the eggs or hatchlings inside. They kept track of the comings and goings of the seagulls for an entire summer. It was a fabulous experience, but one that was topped by her next adventure.

In the summer after her third year in college, Elise was lucky enough to go to Kenya and Tanzania on a four-month study abroad field research trip. During that time, Elise and her fellow research assistants camped in tents on the African savanna.

A savanna is a huge area of land covered by tall grasses. The grasses grow in clumps, and some of them can be as high as 10 feet. There are trees and small shrubs scattered throughout.

Seeing a leopard while studying abroad in Tanzania

Julie Hanta Razafimanahaka

Julie Hanta Razafimanahaka is the director of Madagasikara Voakajy. This organization is leading conservation efforts to protect some of Madagascar's most threatened forests and species.

Julie became interested in conservation when she was only 13 years old and a member of the Girl Guides in Madagascar. The Girl Guides are similar to the Girl Scouts.

What interested Elise the most was the animals. She was working with the local government in Kenya and Tanzania to count the number of animals living freely on the savanna. The government wanted to find a way to manage the animals' range, or the area they traveled, so it could ensure the animals would thrive.

As part of her job, Elise was teamed with four other research assistants and one ranger. Every day, they walked 12 miles, searching for animals. They marked down everything they saw in their notebooks.

At the end of this field project, Elise and her fellow college students made recommendations to the local community about how to improve their conservation efforts. The students suggested ways to better use the region's sanctuaries to benefit the animals.

Julie's love of nature and interest in biodiversity stayed with her throughout her high school and college years. She is very interested in the links between people and nature, and wants to inspire more students to pursue biodiversity conservation.

In 2015, Julie was chosen as the recipient of the Young Women in Conservation Biology Award. It is a prestigious honor recognizing her dedication and determination as she rose from an intern to director of the organization in just 12 years.

> 66 . . . More women should be able to stand up and speak in public about conservation. This will slowly, but certainly, provoke positive changes toward sustainable development and conservation. 99
>
> **—Julie Hanta Razafimanahaka,**
> conservationist, director of Madagasikara Voakajy

Elise did this when she was only 20 years old. This shows that it is not necessary to be older to contribute to a community. Simply have a passion, learn all you can, and be vocal about your support or recommendations. This can make you a good advocate for animals.

Elise's most recent research project involved listening to elephants. She was a part of the Elephant Listening Project that was being conducted in the Cornell University Lab of Ornithology where she was attending college. For this program, Elise spent her time listening to recordings of elephants in Africa. Most of the sounds that elephants make are actually unable to be heard by humans. By using special microphones to capture the sounds, and then enhancing them with electronics, Elise was able to hear the elephants.

She listened to the elephants and took notes on the different sounds she heard. This gave the lead researchers a great deal of information on the size of the elephant population.

They could tell how many elephants were in an area and what the herd was doing. It was even possible to tell the number of male and female elephants just by listening.

Occasionally, Elise could hear illegal loggers or poachers on the microphones. Her work with the Elephant Listening Project was very important. The results were used to help African communities to better manage their wildlife and land use.

Zoologists are not just concerned with the animals themselves, but also the environment in which they live. By doing field research, a zoologist-in-training can learn a great deal about how animals and humans fit into the earth's global ecosystem. This is an important concept.

PS

Listen Up!

You can learn more about the Elephant Listening Project and even listen for yourself at this website! Can you identify different elephant sounds? Do you think if you listened to many different recordings, you'd get better at hearing the sounds? Why is it important to learn about animal language?

elephant listening project 🔍

FIRST JOB!

A love for conservation led to Elise's next step at Vermont Institute of Natural Science (VINS), which rehabilitates migratory birds and raptors. She helped injured birds, including ones shot by hunters or hit by cars, to get them ready to go back out into the wild. Elise spent many hours feeding baby birds. She even had to set her clock to get up every hour in the middle of the night to feed them.

During this job, Elise discovered that, although she likes birds, she really wanted to work with mammals. Mammals are most of the animals found in a zoo—lions, tigers, bears, monkeys, and many others.

Elise left her job with VINS and began working as a zookeeper at the Binghamton Zoo in Binghamton, New York. For this job, she was in charge of cleaning enclosures, feeding animals, training them, keeping them healthy, and enriching their lives.

Elise worked with pretty much every animal in the zoo, from penguins and red pandas to snakes, raptors, and tigers.

She loved it! She particularly loved working with the tigers. Something about these massive animals touched her heart.

While the Binghamton Zoo was an amazing experience, Elise decided that she wanted to work at a bigger zoo. She applied to be a zookeeper at the very prestigious San Diego Zoo Safari Park.

Since it is so popular, the San Diego Zoo Safari Park does not just accept new applicants. To show that she was serious, Elise quit her job at the Binghamton Zoo and went to San Diego, California. She worked as a tour guide at the Safari Park for a year. She guided three different types of tours and learned the layout of the Park, including the locations and habits of the animals there.

In order to get more experience, Elise joined a group called Roar Corps to allow her more access to the larger animals. As a member, she followed an established zookeeper into the enclosures and helped them do their tasks. You guessed it—more cleaning! Elise helped to shovel hundreds of pounds of rhino, deer, and gazelle manure every single day.

BABY TIGERS!

Elise's perseverance paid off. She was hired as a full-time zookeeper at the San Diego Zoo Safari Park. Her current job is working with nine tigers, including raising four tiger cubs. One tiger actually needed to be bottle-fed for the first few months, and Elise took on the job.

Cool Careers:
Wildlife Conservationist

Do you want to help endangered or threatened species? Become a wildlife conservationist. As a wildlife conservationist, you will travel to exotic environments to gather information on endangered species. You will collect data on how these animals live and interact within their habitats. You'll use that data to help build up the populations of these animals. Some ways to do this include breeding programs or suggesting ways for local governments to reduce their impacts upon the local environment.

The tiger cub was 2.5 pounds when he was born, but at one year, he weighed 145 pounds. Tigers grow fast! Elise not only fed him, but trained him to respond to her commands. She helped him get used to getting shots, being checked over by the veterinarians, and opening his mouth for the dentist.

The other three tiger cubs she is helping raise are fed by their mothers. Elise spends most of every day training them and getting them used to her.

Elise has achieved her goal of becoming a zookeeper. Her path required dedication, determination, and long hours of hard, hot, difficult work. But she is now pursuing her lifelong dream. It is a path that any person can achieve if they just keep going.

CHAPTER 4

Erin Seney

Have you ever had a pet that was part of your family? Maybe you wished that you could spend your whole life taking care of your pet. That's what Erin Seney did. Her pet turtle, Dallas, inspired her to become a zoologist who tracks sea turtles. Turtles live very long lives and, more than 25 years later, he's still with her.

Like many budding zoologists, Erin always had pets. She had cats, dogs, a guinea pig, and gerbils. In the first grade, she decided that she wanted to become a veterinarian. She thought this was her best way to help animals.

Taking care of the medical needs of animals is rewarding and important work. But something made Erin reconsider. Instead, Erin decided that she wanted to combine her love of the outdoors with her love of animals.

Erin enjoyed going to her local pond and hanging out to watch the wildlife. It was there that she met her first freshwater turtle. Definitely love at first sight! Erin really wanted a pet turtle, but her parents weren't crazy about the idea. Fortunately, a childhood friend took care of that.

When she was 12 and living in Texas, Erin was given a box turtle by her friend. Luckily, her mom agreed to it and even took her to the store to get all of the supplies. But taking care of the turtle, named Dallas, was Erin's job.

She was thrilled! And Erin has done such an amazing job that 25 years and many different homes later, Dallas is still one of her best friends.

A LIFE OF SCIENCE

Erin's love of science was connected not just with animals, but with all things science. This passion started early. In elementary school, her teacher had the students do long-term projects. One project was to create a terrarium. Terrariums are like aquariums for fish, but they contain plants and sometimes small animals.

Erin's class put hermit crabs in their terrarium. Naturally, when the project was over, Erin was the one to volunteer to bring it home. She wanted to add another animal to her list of pets!

Since her parents were very supportive of science and education, they agreed to keep the hermit crab. Her mom took Erin to the store to get the supplies she needed. The hermit crab lived a happy life among the shells, sand, and tiny plants.

Ask & Answer

Are you the first to raise your hand to volunteer? What kinds of volunteer activities do you like?

Erin's love of science continued into her high school years. She took a lot of science classes and did well in them. She did so well that her chemistry teacher nominated her for a Young Women in Science program.

How to Make a Terrarium

If you want to build a habitat for your hermit crab, you'll need some supplies. Here are some of the things you'll want to have.

- An empty aquarium or other large glass container with a lid.
- Two small bowls for food and water, glass or plastic.
- A heat lamp or under-tank heater (hermit crabs like to be warm).
- A spray bottle with water for keeping the terrarium moist.
- Two empty shells for the hermit crab to grow into as needed.
- Pieces of driftwood, sand, and plastic plants or real ones in soil. These will give the hermit crab places to climb and hide.

Find a book or website that tells you how to take care of your hermit crab. Make sure you have a safe place to put your terrarium, and then sit back and enjoy watching your crab!

When Erin was accepted into the program, she got to take college-level science classes during the summer. It was great fun! Although Erin's teacher might have wanted her to become a chemist, Erin is sure that her teacher is proud that she became a marine biologist instead.

Living near the Chesapeake Bay in Maryland, Erin really enjoyed going to the water and watching the animals she found there—hermit crabs, horseshoe crabs, blue crabs, many different kinds of fish, and, of course, turtles. There are five different kinds of turtles in the Chesapeake Bay, and Erin loved seeing all of them.

When Erin was in high school, she volunteered at the Virginia Institute of Marine Science. She wanted to be around the sea creatures that she loved. Her job? To help feed the animals and clean the aquariums. Perhaps you've noticed that all of these zoologists, at some point in their careers, spent large amounts of time cleaning up after the animals.

Ask & Answer

Do you have a special pet? Do you think that it might inspire you to figure out your future career?

Inspiring Scientists and Teachers

Most female scientists say that, at a young age, they were inspired by a teacher or parent to pursue science. It might have been the science teacher who told them to keep going or who showed them that girls could do anything. Or perhaps it was the parent who took their daughter on camping trips, horseback rides, trips to the ocean, and other outdoor activities.

Now that they are older, many scientists look to inspire their own students. Dr. Mojisola Usikalu, a physicist who received an Elsevier Foundation Award for Women in Science in the Developing World, believes that supporting females interested in science is extremely important.

She is now a teacher herself and serves as a role model for young women in Nigeria. Mojisola urges her female students not to give up. She tells them that they can achieve success as she did through dedication, determination, and hard work.

> 66 When you realize the value of all life, you dwell less on what is past and concentrate more on the preservation of the future. 99
>
> **—Dian Fossey,**
> American zoologist, expert on mountain gorillas

While cleaning up after animals might seem like an unpleasant job, it is a very necessary one. The animals that live in captivity are dependent on their human caretakers to keep them healthy and happy. That job must include cleaning the enclosures where they live.

Think about it. Humans have bathrooms in their homes, but animals do not. All of that waste has to go somewhere. If it's allowed to pile up, it can cause disease.

If zoology is in your future, you had better get used to cleaning up after animals. Start practicing now by offering to clean out your pet's cage or aquarium or scooping up feces in the backyard. It is never too early to start taking proper care of your animals.

COLLEGE BOUND

Despite her interest in the ocean and the animals, Erin picked a university that didn't even have a marine science program. Several of her family members had attended the University of Virginia, and she wanted to continue the family legacy.

She decided to get a degree in biology. Biology is close to zoology. It is the study of life sciences, but focuses more on cells and all life, and less on what she really wanted to study, which was animals.

About halfway through college, Erin decided to add to her biology experience, so she added a minor in environmental science. This allowed her to study ecology and how wildlife interacts with its environment.

Erin found a great way to interact with animals during school. She signed up to help an assistant to a researcher who was working with frogs. Erin's job was to handle the frogs, take samples from them, and care for them in the laboratory.

Dr. Marjorie Brooks

It is definitely possible to turn what you love into a full-blown career. Many of these women have done so, Dr. Marjorie Brooks included. She says that she has been fascinated by the world all around her for as long as she can remember. She was always asking questions, wanting to know more. When she grew older, Marjorie took courses to become a biologist. She was very interested in conservationism, in protecting animals and their ecosystems.

After about a year of taking samples, comparing results, and working completely indoors, Erin had learned a lot. She also knew that working in a laboratory was not something she wanted to do long-term, for a career.

Still, Erin kept going and graduated with a bachelor's degree in biology and an environmental science minor. Now it was time to pursue her real love—working with turtles.

GRADUATE SCHOOL

Erin decided that she could ignore her love of sea turtles no longer. She headed to the College of William & Mary and the Virginia Institute of Marine Science to get her master's degree.

Marjorie has her PhD in biogeochemistry and aquatic ecology and is an associate professor at Southern Illinois University's Department of Zoology. She focuses on the affect that humans have on ocean chemistry and how that impacts the animals that live there. Her recommendations for how to follow your dream to become a zoologist? Go outside! Hike. Garden. Join a local green space group. Participate in a beach cleanup. Watch bugs or birds in your own backyard. Become connected to nature!

Her path to her graduate degree was not without challenges. The first interview with her new advisor was rather interesting. He asked Erin a great deal about her undergraduate work in biology and environmental science. He quizzed her about her research project with the frogs.

Erin had to tell him that it didn't quite go as planned. She had encountered some difficulties with the lab procedures and specimens. Her advisor smiled and explained that it was a good experience for her—now she knew what it was like to fail. He then agreed to accept her as his graduate student.

Rachel Carson

Rachel Carson (1907–1964) graduated from Pennsylvania College for Women (now Chatham College) in 1929. She went on to study at Johns Hopkins University. At that time, not many women were studying marine biology.

Rachel wasn't just a great female scientist, she was also an outspoken activist for environmentalism. She was the first to speak up about the damaging effects of using pesticides and fertilizers. Her book, *Silent Spring*, talked about how ecosystems were being destroyed by pesticides, such as DDT. She was so outspoken and was held in such high regard that the U.S. government listened.

The concept of failure is an important one to learn. Scientists often experience failure, sometimes on a daily basis!

A scientist's hypothesis, or idea, for how an experiment will turn out can be completely wrong. Perhaps they believe an experiment will turn out a certain way, and it does not. Maybe they predict an animal will react with one behavior, and then they don't. It is quite common to fail initially to prove your original idea.

photo credit: U.S. Fish and Wildlife Service

DDT was banned a few years later. Her passion for the environment helped to preserve the world for future generations. You can see Rachel Carson talk about conservation and the balance of nature here. How has conservation changed since she began to speak out against DDT?

Rachel Carson CBS Reports 🔍

The best part about being a scientist is that failure is not a negative thing. Instead, it always teaches you something. You might have heard the saying that you can always learn something from your mistakes. That is completely true for scientists.

Many experiments that failed have ended up creating some amazing products. For example, the creator of the Post-it note was actually trying to make a super-strong adhesive. Instead, he created a multi-million dollar product. Where would we be without Post-It notes? Penicillin, an antibiotic drug used to fight infection, was created by accident, too.

In this case, Erin's "failure" as a lab technician enabled her to understand that she would be much happier working outdoors in the field. That led her to become an outstanding marine biologist.

Ask & Answer

Have you ever failed at something? Did you learn anything from it?

SEA TURTLES

At the Virginia Institute of Marine Science, Erin was finally able to study what she really wanted to learn about—sea turtles! Eager to do anything that involved them, Erin volunteered to take a look at a huge number of samples that had been collected on the sea turtles.

What was she looking at? Their habitats? Their size? Their swimming paths? No. She was examining their stomach contents. Did that stop Erin? Of course not.

She dug into the project and had a lot of fun with it. Her job took her into the field, where she helped collect samples from strandings. These are turtles that wash up onshore after they die. She also collected information on the dead turtles to help researchers better understand them and the threats they might have faced.

Back in the lab, Erin analyzed the stomach contents of the sea turtles to find out what the turtles ate. Her decision to work with sea turtle diets was a good one. The program that Erin began more than 10 years ago was picked up by another organization and is still going strong.

GETTING HER DOCTORATE

Erin went to Texas A&M University to get her doctorate. For her research, she worked on an endangered turtle species called Kemp's ridley sea turtles.

She started a satellite tracking system for turtles. Her work was with the National Marine Fisheries Service

Sea turtles from top: Kemp's ridley, loggerhead, hawksbill

(NMFS), which was involved in rescuing turtles that were caught on hook-and-line fishing gear. After NMFS responded to the call to help turtles and worked with a veterinarian to check for and remove any hooks, the turtles were tagged and released.

Each turtle received two flipper tags. These are on the outside of the flippers. They are harmless to the turtles, but do occasionally come off.

The Importance of Diet

Green turtles eat primarily algae and seagrasses. Loggerhead turtles often eat horseshoe crabs and blue crabs. Leatherback turtles love jellyfish.

Sometimes, if a food source becomes scarce, turtles find other things to eat. For example, during Erin's research for her master's degree, she discovered that many loggerhead turtles in the Chesapeake Bay were eating fish. This was an interesting find, since loggerhead turtles do not normally eat fish.

Why were they eating fish? It was likely because the populations of horseshoe crabs and blue crabs were much smaller than they had been in the past. The loggerheads had to adapt and eat what they could find—and they could find fish in fishing nets.

This information was very helpful to Erin and her team. They learned that in order to get the loggerheads back to their normal eating habits, the conditions for horseshoe crabs and blue crabs must be improved. The people in charge of taking care of the Chesapeake Bay were informed. They could make changes to the water management to help the turtles survive.

The turtles also get an inside tag called a Passive Integrated Transponder, or PIT tag. The PIT tag is inserted into the turtle with a long needle and remains there for the life of the turtle.

The tag can be read when a special electronic reader is passed over it. These PIT tags are the same microchip tags used by veterinarians in dogs. Tagging allows the researchers to identify turtles if they are seen again by other researchers, allowing them to create a "history" for tagged turtles that are recaptured.

Also, as part of her PhD research, Erin was able to attach satellite transmitters to nesting female turtles and some of the hook-caught turtles for tracking. The transmitter is glued on top of the turtle's shell a few inches behind its head. It does not interfere with the turtle's movement in any way, but allows researchers to track its location.

Ask & Answer

Are you interested in doing research and working in a lab or would you rather work outdoors in the field?

Erin with a green sea turtle
photo taken during permitted research conducted by the University of Central Florida

Erin was the first to come up with a way to allow the transmitter to expand and grow slightly with the turtle. This meant the transmitter would stay on the turtle longer.

66 There are so many television shows about koala bears and kittens. All the attention seems focused on a handful of charismatic 'celebrity' animals. Even scientists get less funding for animals that aren't cute and cuddly. In fact, large mammal species appear in 500 times as many published papers as threatened amphibians. 99

—Lucy Cooke,
zoologist

Why track the turtles? Researchers are curious to find out everything they can about the sea turtles. Until this point, marine biologists had little understanding of where Kemp's ridley turtles from the upper Texas coast went.

The data they gathered from signals that were sent to satellites helped them understand the turtles' behavior and habitat. This information was passed to the local and national marine management associations that want to protect this endangered species. It helps them keep the turtles safe and the population growing.

All sea turtles are protected under the Endangered Species Act, and they are listed as either "endangered" or "threatened." This means that sea turtles have low populations and are in danger of becoming extinct.

In learning about turtles' movements, it is also possible for the researchers to determine their habitat. Habitat includes places where the turtles eat, live, and breed. Once the researchers know the location of the habitat, they can better protect it from boats, ships, and motorized jet skis.

After receiving her PhD, Erin set off on her own. She did a policy fellowship at the National Science Foundation and then at the NMFS headquarters. After the fellowship, she stayed on as an independent consultant and continued to work on issues related to marine resources, fish, turtles, and mammals.

WHAT SHE'S DOING NOW

Erin is on the faculty of the University of Central Florida with the Marine Turtle Research Group. She is responsible for running two field programs. One program monitors the nesting beaches along 30 miles of central Florida. The turtles she and the research teams observe are loggerhead, green, and leatherback turtles. They also do a year-long in-water program where they capture turtles with safe nets so that they can inspect, measure, weigh, and tag them.

The turtles are not harmed when the researchers capture them. They use nets with buoys on top. When the buoys are pulled down and can't be seen, that means there is probably a turtle in the net. Since the turtles require air to breathe, the nets are monitored constantly.

The researchers handle the turtles as gently as possible. They tag and weigh them, and even take tissue and blood samples. This is to determine the turtle's health and genetics, or which nesting population it came from.

The research is a way to track populations and see how big the groups are getting. The goal is to understand how to help protect these amazing animals.

Are you interested in turtles and other sea creatures? Erin suggests looking for educational outreach programs at camps, science clubs, and local aquariums.

Check out any local museums or aquatic programs that allow you to volunteer behind the scenes, even if it is just cleaning enclosures. Any opportunity that lets you do hands-on interaction with animals is great.

Ask & Answer

What do you find appealing about working with animals? What skills do you have that might make you a good zoologist?

You can also get involved by being eco-friendly in everything you do. Recycle. Eliminate your use of plastics and use reusable bags. Plastics can end up in the ocean and do great harm to the animals. Make responsible choices about the seafood you eat.

Be a friend to the earth. This will show not only your love of animals but also your love of the planet.

Cool Careers:
Marine Mammal Trainer

Do you love working with animals? Try being a marine mammal trainer! With a degree in zoology and some training, you can learn to work with animals. You should like exercise, since most likely you will be doing a lot of swimming. A love of fish is good—handling it, not eating it—since you may be using many fish to reward your marine mammals. With lots of hard work, you could have a dolphin eating out of your hand and jumping, diving, and even speaking to you.

Timeline

384–322 BCE

- Aristotle, the "father of biology" and zoology is the first to classify animals.
- Pythias of Assos, wife of Aristotle, is the first female zoologist.

23 CE

- Pliny the Elder writes a series of books called *Historia Naturalis*, or *Natural History*.

160

- Claudius Galen develops the study of anatomy and physiology of animals.

1248

- Saint Albertus Magnus studies Aristotle's work and writes about animals. His teachings endure for several hundred years.

1551

- Konrad von Gesner writes the first modern book on zoology called *Historia Animalium* (*History of the Animals*).

1700s

- Carl Linnaeus creates a taxonomic system of classifying animals.

1842

- English paleontologist Richard Owen coins the phrase "dinosaur" for the reptiles that lived between about 200 and 65 million years ago.

1856

- Austrian monk Gregor Mendel establishes the science of genetics, about how animals and plants inherit traits from their parents.

1859

- Charles Darwin publishes *On the Origin of Species by Means of Natural Selection*, which explains the theory of evolution.

1900

- Dr. Cornelia Clapp earns the first and second biology doctorates awarded to a woman in the United States, from Syracuse and Chicago Universities.

1940

- Dr. Roger Arliner Young becomes the first African American female to earn a doctorate in zoology, from the University of Chicago.

1941

- Zoologist Rachel Carson publishes her first book on the ocean to educate people on the undersea environment and the animals that live there.

1953

- Marine biologist Eugenie Clark ("The Shark Lady") publishes her first book on her research titled *Lady with a Spear*.

1960

- Dame Jane Goodall arrives in Africa and begins studying Gombe Stream chimpanzees.

1966

- Dian Fossey goes to Tanzania to study the gorillas.

1986

- Zoologist Terri Irwin starts a rehabilitation center for cougars.

1990

- Marine biologist and explorer Dr. Sylvia Earle becomes the first female chief scientist of the National Oceanic and Atmospheric Association (NOAA).

1992

- Zoologists Steve and Terri Irwin start the *Crocodile Hunter* TV series to bring attention to animals in the wild.

1996

- Zoologists Chris and Martin Kratt start a television show called *Kratts' Creatures* to show kids how animals live in the wild.

2006

- Terri Irwin, naturalist and widow of the late crocodile hunter Steve Irwin, is awarded an Honorary Member in the General Division of the Order of Australia for her "outstanding dedication to wildlife conservation and the tourism industry."

2012

- Zoologist Lucy Cooke produces a series of viral videos featuring the sloth, and introduces thousands of viewers to an animal they'd never considered before. For this work, she is awarded the National Geographic Emerging Explorer Award.

Introduction

- Why is zoology an important career for women and men? What would science be like if only one gender worked at it?

Chapter 1

- If you could pick any animal to study, what would it be? Would you want to study in a laboratory or go out into the field?

- What do you dream of doing? Does it include studying animals? How will you overcome any obstacles that come your way?

- Are you interested in studying animals? Does one species of animals capture your attention more than others? Do you want to know how an animal lives, acts, and behaves in nature?

Chapter 2

- What activities do you love to do now? Do you ever think that they might lead you to a certain career?

- Are you willing to change your mind to follow your own path? Even if it takes you in a different direction from your original one?

- Is there a topic that you are passionate about? What can you do to tell people about it? How can you get others involved in helping?

Chapter 3

- Have you ever really wanted something that you had to work for? What did you do to learn more about it?

- Do you have a teacher or parent who supports what you are interested in? Do they inspire you to want to pursue your dreams? How does that make you feel?

- Have you ever had a job that you didn't like? Did you learn anything from it?

- What can you do in your area to help with conservation? How can you help to improve your environment?

- How are animals treated in your community? Is there anything that needs to change? What can you do to help bring awareness and address the problem?

Chapter 4

- Are you the first to raise your hand to volunteer? What kinds of volunteer activities do you like?

- Do you have a special pet? Do you think that it might inspire you to figure out your future career?

- Have you ever failed at something? Did you learn anything from it?

- Are you interested in doing research and working in a lab or would you rather work outdoors in the field?

- What do you find appealing about working with animals? What skills do you have that might make you a good zoologist?

accolade: an award or special honor for doing good work.

accurate: true, correct.

adapt: to change to survive in new or different conditions.

advocate: to publicly support something.

algae: a simple organism found in water. It is like a plant but does not have roots, stems, or leaves.

altitude: the height above the level of the sea. Also called elevation.

amphibian: an animal with moist skin that is born in water but lives on land. An amphibian changes its body temperature by moving to warmer or cooler places. Frogs, toads, newts, efts, and salamanders are amphibians.

analyze: breaking down problems into small parts to find solutions.

ancestor: someone from your family or culture who lived before you.

anthropologist: a person who studies anthropology, the study of human culture and development.

applied field: a field of study in which a scientist uses what they learn to solve specific problems.

aquatic: living or growing in water.

awareness: able to observe or notice something.

BCE: put after a date, BCE stands for Before Common Era and counts years down to zero. CE stands for Common Era and counts years up from zero. This book was published in 2017 CE.

binomial nomenclature: using two terms to classify an organism.

biochemistry: the study of chemistry in living things.

biodiversity: the range of living things in an ecosystem.

biogeochemistry: the study of how chemicals are transferred between living systems and the environment.

biologist: a scientist who studies living things.

biology: the study of living things.

botanist: a scientist who studies plant life.

botany: the study of plants.

breed: to produce babies.

burrow: to dig under.

cell: the basic unit or part of a living thing. Cells are so small they can only be seen with a microscope.

Glossary

chemical: the pure form of a substance. Some chemicals can be combined or broken up to create new chemicals.

chemistry: the science of the properties of substances and how substances react with one another.

classify: to put things in groups based on what they have in common.

climate: the weather patterns in an area during a long period of time.

climate change: a change in the long-term average weather patterns of a place.

coexist: to live together.

community: all the living things within a region that interact with each other.

comprehensive: complete, detailed.

conservation: managing and protecting natural resources.

critical thinking: involving careful examination and judgment.

crops: plants grown for food and other uses.

data: information from tests or experiments.

descendant: a person related to someone who lived in the past.

doctorate: a PhD, the highest degree awarded by a graduate school.

ecology: the study of the interaction between organisms and their environment.

encyclopedia: a book or set of books giving information on many subjects or on many aspects of one subject and typically arranged alphabetically.

endangered: a plant or animal species with a dangerously low population.

entomologist: a scientist who studies insects.

environment: everything in nature, living and nonliving, including plants, animals, soil, rocks, and water.

erosion: the gradual wearing away of rock or soil by water and wind.

ethical: acting in a way that upholds someone's belief in right and wrong.

ethics: whether something is right or wrong.

evolution: changing gradually during many years.

evolve: a change in a species of living things over time in response to the world around it.

expedition: a trip taken by a group of people for a specific purpose such as exploration, scientific research, or war.

extinct: when a group of plants or animals dies out and there are no more left in the world.

feces: poop.

fellowship: payment for research work at a university for a period of time.

field: a place to do research out in the natural world rather than in a laboratory.

fisheries: areas where fish are caught.

fossil: the remains of any organism, including animals and plants, that have been preserved in rock.

fossil fuels: three forms of fuel that we can burn for energy—oil, natural gas, and coal. They formed more than 300 million years ago from tiny fossils of plants and animals. When we use it up, fossil fuels will be gone forever.

function: how something works. To work or operate in a particular, correct way.

gender: male or female, and their roles or behavior defined by society.

genetics: the study of how traits are passed from one generation to the next through genes.

genus: the general name of an animal family. One of the categories into which all living things can be classified.

geologist: a scientist who studies the history and the physical nature of the earth.

habitat: the natural area where a plant or an animal lives.

herpetologist: a scientist who studies reptiles and amphibians.

hypothesis: a prediction or unproven idea that tries to explain certain facts or observations.

inspire: to fill with the urge or ability to do or feel something, especially to do something creative.

interact: when things that are together affect each other.

interaction: how things work together.

interconnect: when two or more things have an impact on each other.

intrigue: to arouse the curiosity or interest of someone.

Glossary

invasive: a species that is not native to an ecosystem and that is harmful to the ecosystem in some way.

Latin: the language of ancient Rome and its empire.

legacy: the lasting influence of a person or thing.

mammal: a warm-blooded animal, such as a human, dog, or cat, that can keep itself warm. Mammals feed milk to their young and usually have hair or fur covering most of their skin.

manure: the poop from farm and zoo animals.

marine: found in the ocean.

marsh: an inland area of wet, low land.

master's degree: an advanced degree from a college or university that represents mastery in a specific field of study.

migration: moving from one place to another, often with the change in seasons.

natural resource: a material or substance such as gold, wood, and water that occurs in nature and is valuable to humans.

natural selection: the process that allows organisms best adapted for an environment to reproduce.

naturalist: a person who studies nature.

Nobel Prize: an annual prize in the sciences, literature, medicine, and peace, established by Alfred Nobel.

nocturnal: active at night.

observation: something you notice.

organism: any living thing, such as a plant or animal.

ornithology: the study of birds.

perseverance: a continued effort to do something even in the face of failure or opposition.

pesticide: a chemical used to kill pests, such as insects.

PhD: stands for Doctor of Philosophy. A PhD is the highest degree in an area of study given by a college or university.

physician: a doctor.

physicist: a scientist who studies matter, energy, and forces.

physics: the study of physical forces, including matter, energy, and motion, and how these forces interact with each other.

poacher: someone who hunts or fishes illegally.

policy: a system of principles used to guide decisions.

population: all of the people (or plants or animals) in an area or in a group.

predator: an animal that hunts another animal for food.

prediction: what you think will happen.

prestigious: something inspiring respect and admiration.

primatologist: a scientist who studies primates. These are mammals that have large brains, nails on the hands and feet, and a short snout. Apes, monkeys, chimpanzees, and humans are primates.

profile: a story about someone.

pure field: an area of study in which scientists are interested in learning about a topic for the sole purpose of gathering information.

raptor: a bird of prey, such as an eagle, hawk, falcon, or owl, that hunts other animals.

reptile: an animal covered with scales that crawls on its belly or on short legs. A reptile changes its body temperature by moving to warmer or cooler places. Snakes, turtles, lizards, alligators, and crocodiles are reptiles.

research: the planned investigation and study of something to discover facts and reach conclusions.

rigorous: extremely thorough and disciplined.

role model: someone who is an inspiration.

sanctuary: a place of safety, where wildlife is protected.

satellite: a device that orbits the earth to relay communication signals or transmit information.

savanna: a dry, rolling grassland with scattered shrubs and trees.

scientific method: the way scientists ask questions and do experiments to try to prove their ideas.

social welfare: the health and well-being of members of a society.

Glossary

species: a group of plants or animals that are closely related and produce offspring.

statistics: numbers that show facts about a subject.

sustainable: when resources are used in a way that does not use them up.

taxonomy: the branch of science concerned with classification.

technology: the tools, methods, and systems used to solve a problem or do work.

theory: an unproven idea used to explain something.

thesis: a statement or theory that is put forward as an idea to be proved. Also a long research paper written for a degree, such as a master's degree or doctorate.

threatened: a plant or animal species whose existence is at risk.

tidal: having to do with the daily rise and fall of ocean water.

tissue: a large number of cells in an organism that are similar in form and function and grouped together, such as muscle tissue.

track: to follow an animal to find them.

trait: a feature or quality that makes somebody or something recognizable.

transmitter: the part of a radio or satellite that sends signals.

veterinarian: an animal doctor.

watershed: the land area that drains into a river or a lake.

wetland: a low area filled with water such as a marsh or swamp.

wilderness: land that is not settled or changed by people.

wildlife: animals, birds, and other living things that live wild in nature.

wildlife rehabilitator: a zoologist who cares for sick, injured, or orphaned animals.

zoologist: a person who studies animals.

zoology: the study of animals.

Books

- *Everything You Need to Know about Animals: A First Encyclopedia for Budding Zoologists.* Davies, Nicola. Kingfisher, 2013.

- *Be a Zoologist (Be a Scientist!).* Belton, Blair. Gareth Stevens Publishing, 2014.

- *Dian Fossey: Friend to Africa's Gorillas.* Doak, Robin S. Heinemann Library, 2014.

- *Time for Kids Magazine. Time for Kids Book of How - All about Animals.* Time for Kids, 2014.

- *The Elephant Scientist.* O'Connell, Caitlin; Jackson, Donna M.; and Rodwell, T. C. Houghton Mifflin for Children, 2011.

- *Last of the Giants: The Rise and Fall of Earth's Most Dominant Species.* Campbell, Jeff. Zest, 2016.

- *Zoologists and Ecologists (Out of the Lab: Extreme Jobs in Science.* Owen, Ruth. PowerKids Press. 2013.

- *Zoology for Kids: Understanding and Working with Animals, with 21 Activities* (For Kids series) Hestermann, Josh. Chicago Review Press. 2015.

- *Zoologists in the Field.* Spilsbury, Louise. Capstone, 2010.

Resources

Websites

- Bioscience Careers: Zoologist
  aboutbioscience.org/careers/zoologist

- HomeschoolFreestuff Animals! Zoology
  *homeschoolfreestuff.wordpress.com/
  science/biology/zoology-animals*

- Go Abroad: Zoology and Wildlife Internships Abroad
  *goabroad.com/intern-abroad/search/zoology-
  wildlife-sciences/internships-abroad-1*

- San Diego Zoo Kids
  kids.sandiegozoo.org

- Science Buddies: Zoologist and Wildlife Biologist
  *sciencebuddies.org/science-engineering-careers/
  life-sciences/zoologist-and-wildlife-biologist*

- Smithsonian's National Zoo and Conservation Biology
  Institute
  nationalzoo.si.edu

- St. Louis Zoo: So You Want to be a Zookeeper?
  stlzoo.org/animals/soyouwanttobeazookeeper

- University of Michigan Museum of Zoology
  lsa.umich.edu/ummz

- Veterinarian Technician: Top Blogs about Zoology
  veterinariantechnician.org/top-45-zoology-and-zoo-blogs

- American Museum of Natural History: What is Zoology?
  amnh.org/explore/ology/zoology

- The Dian Fossey Gorilla Fund International
  800 Cherokee Avenue, SE
  Atlanta, Georgia 30315
  1-800-851-0203
  gorillafund.org

Resources

QR Code Glossary

- Page 9: perseus.tufts.edu/hopper/ text?doc = Plin. + Nat. + toc
- Page 20: enzoology.com
- Page 35: conservationbytes.com/2010/08/26/ what-is-biodiversity-video
- Page 65: birds.cornell.edu/brp/elephant
- Page 81: youtube.com/watch?v = 8nriVjC0H8I

Index